T0193466

Everyday Miracles

Tales of Life *Beyond* Life

Bonney Rega

iUniverse, Inc.
Bloomington

Everyday Miracles
Tales of Life *Beyond* Life

Cover design by Julio Granda and Julia Bunn

iUniverse books may be ordered through booksellers or by contacting:

iUniverse
1663 Liberty Drive
Bloomington, IN 47403
www.iuniverse.com
1-800-Authors (1-800-288-4677)

ISBN: 978-1-4759-7560-4 (sc)
ISBN: 978-1-4759-7562-8 (e)

Library of Congress Control Number: 2013902493

Printed in the United States of America

iUniverse rev. date: 03/13/2013

Contents

Introduction

Mysticism to the mystic is both
science and religion.

Hazrat Inayat Khan

According to our most forward-thinking physicists, including Stephen Hawking, Leonard Susskind, Michio Kaku, and Brian Greene, our universe contains at least eleven dimensions, and it either parallels or intersects many other universes. Life is far more complex and mysterious than we ever imagined. Of course, long before science became a modern religion, mystics throughout the ages described various planes of existence. And what mystics described as levels of vibration (or "vibes," as they were later dubbed by the hippies) are now being explained as a "theory of everything" called string theory, which unifies the microcosm with the macrocosm. According to string theory everything in the universe, from the smallest atom to the largest galaxy, is made of very tiny vibrating "strings." We are, too. In other words, we humans are all connected through our vibes. Our cells vibrate at a rate that is sympathetic with that of the earth's vibration, while the other planets vibrate at other rates—but the strings are at the bottom of it all! They connect us to one another. Our personal magnetic fields are measurable, as are the planets' and galaxies' magnetic fields—and amazingly tiny, immeasurable strings propel them all. If our ears could only hear the sounds of these strings, we'd be hearing the music of the spheres! String theory remains a theory, since so far we haven't the scientific equipment to truly identify these one-dimensional, smaller-than-subatomic particles. But in the future, near or distant, some clever scientist will invent a measuring device.

These vibrating strings and extra dimensions, universes, and planes can help explain the stories in this book, which tell of unseen beings and loved ones who choose to make their presence seen or heard or felt in unique ways. These disembodied souls appear in dreams, in hunches, or in this shared, waking existence we call "reality." And they often have a sense of humor.

As a hospice chaplain, I've been privileged to be present with, and act as a midwife to, those who are about to cross the great divide into the next level of existence. Sitting in vigil with dying patients creates a sacred space where patients and family members can share their most profound experiences—sometimes tearfully, sometimes quietly, and sometimes joyously. These stories—all of them true—tell of departed souls who comfort their loved ones, of angels and guides who impart wisdom and wit, and of archetypal beings who tease and teach those who reach out to them. There are examples of people who have learned to listen to that still, small intuitive voice, and descriptions of loving, soul-to-soul communications that encourage personal transformation and a deeper understanding of the soul's journey. These tales come from my hospice patients, their families, my coworkers, my friends, and me—we want to share our stories so they can inspire and comfort others. For privacy reasons I have changed names whenever requested. In all other respects, however, these stories are true, including my own. We all come into this life with different talents; one of mine is being able to act as an occasional bridge to those on the other side. Some of my stories are funny or quirky because I have a quirky sense of humor.

Even though our culture doesn't particularly value stories like these, people keep having unusual experiences despite this cultural indifference and sometimes despite downright hostility. In the privacy of my grief groups, I've found that participants are eager to share their remarkable stories of life after life—and sometimes life before life.

Those close to death often talk of "going home." Selma, for example, a patient of mine whose mental capacities were diminishing due to Alzheimer's disease, knew there was something wrong. Looking around at the other residents in the nursing home's activity room, she said, "Go get 'em— they're going home. They wanna go home."

"What about you, Selma?" I asked. "What do you want?"

"I wish I could go with them. I wanna go home, too. I will. Soon." Some months later, she did.

And then there was another Alzheimer's patient, Jan, who was in the end stages of the disease. Jan was normally uncommunicative: she rarely made eye contact and hardly ever spoke. When she did, it was a senseless monologue, a verbal tossed salad. During one visit, however, she surprised me by gazing around the dining room and then looking straight into my eyes and saying, "They're all getting on the bus."

"Who?" I asked.

"You know—all of them." She gestured around the room, where the other patients were sitting at tables.

"What about you, Jan—are you getting on the bus?" I asked.

"No, of course not!" she said. "It's not *my* time to get on the bus, you know. When I'm ready, I'll go." Then she smiled, her eyes glazed over, and she stopped talking. Several months later, ready to go, she did "get on the bus."

What's powerful about these two stories is that whether the women talk about "getting on the bus" (an often-used metaphor) or "going home," on some very deep level they know that they and the other patients are going to die soon. Although they are disoriented and uncommunicative about everything else in their lives, they are focused on their own and others' imminent passing, and they reach up from the depths of their souls' knowledge to talk about it. In the following stories we'll see that "going home" takes many forms.

You've probably wondered, as I have, about what happens when we cross the river from this life to eternity. (The river is yet another metaphor often used by dying people. So are trains, planes, and golden chariots.) We don't really know what happens to folks once they've crossed that river. Do they create their own reality, their own version of heaven or hell? These questions have been pondered throughout the ages. It does seem that consciousness continues in another form: people who've had near-death or out-of-body experiences relate that family members, friends, or religious figures greeted them once they pierced the "veil." Elizabeth Kübler-Ross, the pioneer in this work, has thoroughly documented this cross-cultural phenomenon.

We rarely get firsthand stories of the ongoing existence of disembodied souls, so when we do it is important to share them. What's certain from my experiences of discarnate souls who've connected with others and me is that they have fun. They clearly enjoy eternity, but they also have work to do.

This book is divided into categories describing various forms of spiritual communication so we can share a common vocabulary about the way souls who don't happen to be in bodies contact us from beyond time and space. Because these experiences are themselves multidimensional, some stories contain overlapping elements. Life is complicated. So is spirituality.

Chapter 1

Dreams

To sleep, perchance to dream …

William Shakespeare

One of the most common ways people connect from the other side is through dreams. The dreams through which souls contact their living loved ones are very different from ordinary dreams. They are vivid and rational—things happen in proper sequence, as opposed to the topsy-turvy sequences of everyday, run-of-the-mill dreams, and they are generally suffused with light. The dreamer remembers them; they don't fade as soon as the dreamer awakens. These dreams aren't just realistic; they also often impart information.

At the Bus

In a very lucid dream of mine, my long-dead mother, Minnie, appeared and told me that she was helping people who'd been killed in a bus crash to make the transition to the afterlife. A tiny river separated us, and I watched as she gently helped people's souls leave their bodies so they could move on. When I attempted to cross over, she shooed me away impatiently, just as she might have done in "real" life. She said she was really busy.

"This is my work now," she said. "I just wanted you to know what I'm doing. But you have to stay on your side of the river." So I stayed on my side of the river—but at some point we *all* have to cross the river, don't we?

When I awoke I heard on the morning news about a bus crash in which most of the elderly occupants had been killed. That river crossing was indeed busy.

Millie's Dad

When Millie's father died, she stayed at her mother's home to help ease her loneliness. At week's end, Millie's father appeared to her in a dream and said, "Go to your mother. She's making herself sick worrying. I told her when I died I'd give her a sign I was okay by tweaking her toes in the middle of the night. Well, she's been sitting up in bed every night, scared that I would keep my promise. She's not sleeping at all. She'll make herself so sick she'll die, too, so tell her I won't tweak her toes. It's not her time to die."

Millie walked down the hallway to her mother's room. It was 3:00 a.m., but there was a sliver of light under the bedroom door. Millie knocked. "Come in," said her mom. When Millie entered, she discovered her mother sitting upright in bed, her eyes wide open. She looked terrified.

Millie sat down on the edge of the bed. "Ma, Pa came to visit me in a dream. He said to tell you to go to sleep; you're making yourself sick. And he promised not to tweak your toes."

Her mother burst into tears. "That was our secret—we never told anyone. Now I feel awful. He'll think I don't love him."

Millie said, "He knows you love him. He just doesn't want you to scare yourself to death."

Her mother calmed down and finally slept. Millie returned to her own home the next day, secure that her dad was watching out for her mom. And her mom was relieved, knowing he wasn't going to tweak her toes.

Stella's Healing Journey

Stella, only forty-five years old, had been diagnosed with terminal cancer. A tumor had invaded all the main arteries and nerves in her groin, and no treatment was available. After meditating, praying, and soul-searching for weeks, she felt she had to surrender to the idea that her life was coming to an end. One night, after finally having reached a peaceful state, she fell sound asleep and had a vivid dream in which an all-enveloping light appeared and said, "If you choose, you can survive." It then told her how.

Stella awoke the next morning determined to question the doctors about creating a bypass in her groin that would skirt around the tumor. The solution in her dream became a reality when the doctors reassessed her case and came up with a risky bypass technique that had never been done before but might solve her problem. They were willing to perform the operation if Stella were willing to risk it—

everyone knew she could die during the procedure. The operation was successful, and some twenty years later, Stella said, "I had to surrender to death in order to experience the luminous dream that offered me the way to my healing. Surrendering to death gave me renewed life."

Boy of My Dreams

Stella's dream life continued to inform her. She had a series of vivid dreams about a little blond, blue-eyed boy who would appear to her in one dream and then disappear in another. The dreams were so disturbing that she discussed them with a close friend. She wondered what the dreams meant. Was her son's wife pregnant? If so, why did the child appear and disappear?

Stella's son Mark and his wife Lilli lived in California. They already had two children, and as far as they were concerned, their family was complete. However, there was a little soul hovering around them who had other ideas. Lilli became pregnant, and because for personal reasons the couple was trying to decide whether or not to terminate the pregnancy, they did not tell their parents. When the couple finally decided not to terminate, they shared their original dilemma with Stella, who was relieved.

"That explained the dreams, and the conflict," Stella later said.

Stella was present at the baby's birth, and when she held the blond, blue-eyed boy in her arms, he stared straight into her eyes and she felt a shock of recognition flowing between them. Now that he is over three years old, and beloved by his parents, sisters, and grandparents, he still has a special bond with the grandma whom he visited while he was but a tiny embryo. And he looks exactly like the child of her dreams.

Mother Knows Best

Two sisters, Carol and Charlotte, were members of my grief group because their mother, Pam, had died two months earlier after a brief but deadly illness. In addition to mourning their mother, the women were very upset with their father, who had begun dating a woman shortly after Pam's death. The woman, who had been staying with a next-door neighbor during Pam's illness, pounced at the opportunity to offer help, casseroles, and, finally, condolences. Carol and Charlotte felt the woman was taking advantage of their dad's vulnerability, and they were seriously dismayed when he invited her to move into what they still viewed as their mother's home. They were especially disturbed when their dad drank excessively with his new partner; they felt he was avoiding grieving by bringing her into his home to fill the gap left by Pam's loss.

The sisters tried to share their feelings with their father, but he refused to listen. He expected them to accept the usurper with open hearts and arms, and he also expected his daughters and their children to continue visiting him and swimming in the family pool, just as they had always done. Carol and Charlotte said they couldn't condone their dad's behavior, and they cut off all contact with him, causing extreme pain on all sides. The sisters were certain that Pam would have been angry and mortified if she had known of her husband's actions. However, Pam appeared in dreams to both women independently, saying cheerfully that she didn't give a damn that he'd moved in with another woman and encouraging them to let go of their anger.

Charlotte said, "We're still not happy with the arrangement, but Carol and I have vented our feelings with both our dad and his live-in lover, and we're patching up our relationships with him." The grandkids are delighted to spend time with their grandfather (and to swim in the pool again). It's an uneasy truce: the father's relationship will unfold one way or another, and either way, it's not in the sisters' control. But because Pam told them in no uncertain terms to let it go, they are trying to do so.

Mom, Dad Needs Help!

Julia worried about her dad, Mac, who was so depressed at the loss of his wife that he wept almost constantly for two months following her death. Julia, a health-care worker, knew this went beyond normal grief. She begged her dad to go for psychological help, but he refused, saying, "I can take care of myself." Mac and his wife, both born in Scotland, shared an independent streak. Julia prayed to her mom, Maggie, to help her dad through his depression.

When Julia visited her dad the next afternoon, he said, "Your mother came to me last night in a dream. It was so real. She was partying with all her dead Scottish friends and relatives, as well as mine! You know, Julia, your mother was enjoying herself, singing and dancing and laughing, and she waved good-bye to me. I think she was telling me she's moved on." Now that Mac knew Maggie was among loving friends and relatives, his extreme depression lifted.

Julia, grateful for Mac's healing, was convinced that her mother had played a substantial role in it. When Julia returned to her home, she not only felt Maggie's presence, she also smelled a strong, familiar scent—her mother's distinctive perfume. As Julia says, "The nose knows."

Man of My Dreams

Vera, an American Methodist missionary, was sent to Java in November 1923 to teach at a Methodist-funded school for young girls. She had already reconciled herself to being an "old maid," since she never expected to marry. In order to communicate with her students, she studied Dutch and Malay, and she lived with a native family for eight months to learn the dialect. The Javanese family's ancestors were headhunters; they lived in very primitive conditions. Vera felt lonely and isolated.

In 1929 Vera and another female missionary traveled to Egypt and the Holy Land without male companions—a very courageous thing to do at that time. Vera was an intrepid warrior for Christ, and she fully trusted that he would guide her through all life's difficulties. After spending some time back in the United States, Vera returned to Indonesia and went to Sumatra for a conference of regional missionaries. The night before the meeting, she had what she described as "a very vivid dream." She was on her knees, scrubbing the floor in a native-built hut, when her eyes were drawn to the light-filled doorway. Standing there, illuminated, was a fair-haired young man with brilliant blue eyes. They made eye contact, and she knew immediately that he was to be her husband. Their hearts, minds, and souls connected: this was the mate God intended for her.

The next day, while attending the regional conference, Vera was introduced to the same young man she had seen in her dream—fair-haired, blue-eyed, and, to her, "electric." The Swedish-born Egon was instantly smitten, too.

The Methodist Church in Sweden had sent Egon to Sumatra to work with Chinese refugees from the Sino-Japanese war—they were largely Sumatra's merchant class. Egon was fluent in Chinese, having studied in China for eight months. When he eventually established a church in Sumatra, the congregants became his good friends as well as his parishioners.

Egon proposed to Vera shortly after they met, and of course she said yes. Six months later, they were married. During the next twelve years, they had three children, and survived the Japanese occupation of Sumatra during the war. Because she was the wife of a Swedish national and named on her husband's passport, the Japanese thought she was Swedish, and they allowed both missionaries to visit English and Dutch detainees in the internment camps. Egon and Vera smuggled in drugs, food, and clothing to the half-starved inhabitants, many of whom died despite the couple's efforts. In fact, Egon and Vera's family was half-starved, too.

After the war, Vera, who was in ill health, went back to the States with their children. She urged Egon to leave, also, but he said he had some unfinished business to handle. Knowing he was impulsive, she begged him to join the family, but he again refused.

Unfortunately, Vera's foreboding was prophetic. After she left, Egon went on a Red Cross mission to the village of Tebing Tinggi. His friends had warned him not to go, telling him the trip was too dangerous because extremists were attempting to overthrow the government and were terrorizing the villagers. He went anyway, without explaining why he felt so compelled.

Egon's secret? He knew that in Tebing Tinggi there was a list of Chinese merchants whose donations had paid for the medicine and food he and Vera had smuggled into the Japanese internment camps. The extremists wanted the list, and if they found it they would murder everyone on it. Egon could not let that happen to his friends and parishioners, and so, risking his life, he went to Tebing Tinggi. He successfully destroyed the list, but just as his train departed, he was taken from the platform by two extremists. Vera's fears were justified—Egon was killed.

Vera raised their children on her own and sent all three to college, although she never made more than a hundred dollars a week working for the church. She later published a book about her husband entitled *O Bok Su: The Story of Egon Ostrom, Known to the Chinese as "O Bok Su," an Ambassador of the Kingdom of God*. It was a best seller in Sweden, where Egon is considered a hero. He most certainly was—and so was his American wife.

Space-Time Travel

Margarita, a registered nurse, had a patient named Harry, who was dying of AIDS.

"We became friends," Margarita said. "Harry was a delightful person and kept his sense of humor throughout his illness." At one point during their relationship, Harry shared the following experience with her:

He had called his friend Kelly, who had moved to New Mexico, to tell her he couldn't visit her in her new home as planned—he was too busy dying. That evening he had a very vivid dream: he flew to New Mexico, entered Kelly's home, stepped into the foyer, and walked slowly through the house, remarking on her decorating. It was a thoroughly enjoyable visit. When he woke up, he called Kelly and told her the details of the dream.

"I can't believe it—you've described my house perfectly!" Kelly said. "How did you do that?"

"I don't know," Harry said. "The dream was so real. I loved your decorating, and your house—I felt like I was there. Maybe it's because I'm so close to dying. Anyway, I'm glad I could visit. And I didn't even have to pay for a plane ticket!"

When he told Margarita about the dream later, he asked her, "Do you think souls can fly?"

"It looks like yours did, Harry," she said. "Souls aren't earthbound. That's why you could travel beyond space and time."

Family Reunion

Colleen and Peter were blessed with eleven children. They also had a stillborn son, whom they named James. Although he was born when they were a very young couple, Colleen and Peter always remembered James, cherishing the son they never knew. Over the years their family grew and grew; eventually their descendants included grandchildren, great-grandchildren, and a great-great-grandchild.

They had been married for sixty-eight years when Peter became gravely ill. Colleen was determined to care for him, and so, with the help of several of her children who lived nearby, she kept him at home. Shortly after he entered hospice care, Peter died, surrounded by his children. They sustained one another and supported their mother during their grief.

Several days later, as Colleen was preparing to leave the house for the wake, Peter's sister Michaela arrived and asked, "Have you seen Peter?"

"Yes, I have," Colleen replied. "How did you know?"

"Oh, you went to the wake early," Michaela said.

"No, I haven't been to the wake yet," Colleen said. "Peter came to me in a dream last night. It was so vivid. A bright light surrounded him. He looked healthy and happy. He was holding baby James, and a huge shaft of light shone directly on the baby."

Michaela said, "I had a Mass said for Peter at my church." She handed the Mass card to Colleen, who was startled to see the painting on the face of the card: it showed the Virgin Mary holding baby Jesus in the same way that Peter had held baby James in her dream. A bright shaft of light shone on the infant. "Turn the card over," Michaela said, smiling. "The Mass was said at St. James church."

Several weeks after the funeral, Colleen was diagnosed with incurable cancer. The family was devastated. "Before Peter died, I told him to meet me when it was my time to go," Colleen said. "I didn't know it was going to be so soon." She was, however, comforted to know that she would be reunited with both Peter and the son she never knew.

A Great Friend, a Great-Grandma, and a Gorilla

Lori and her friend Dan used to joke about being related because both of them were descended from Russian Jews. They were proud of their ancestry, and Dan and his wife even adopted a Russian child. Unfortunately, Dan's time with his child was cut short: Dan discovered he had pancreatic cancer. After the diagnosis, he held on to life as long as he could for his daughter, wife, family, and friends. His illness was difficult for him and his loved ones.

Shortly after his death, Lori dreamed of Dan doubled over in pain. "You're dead," she told him. "There's no more pain here—you can stand up." Dan straightened up and smiled. "Now what do I do?" he asked. At that moment Lori's long-dead great-grandmother Rachel appeared with a clipboard. Lori had known her in life as an elderly, white-haired woman, quite round and pillowy. But in the afterlife Rachel was young, slim, and beautiful. "I'm here to guide you," she said to Dan. "My job is routing people to the proper heavenly plane." And the two walked off together.

Lori is sure that Dan is in good hands. Grandma Rachel, who was known for her wise advice in life, is apparently a good guide in the afterlife as well.

Dan never appeared in one of Lori's dreams again, but he found another way to send her a message. Ten years before his death, he and his wife gave Lori an adopt-a-gorilla gift plaque, which she has kept on a shelf in her bathroom ever since. Perfume bottles and other items sit in front of the plaque, which is firmly perched on the shelf. After Lori's dream, the plaque twice jumped off the shelf, falling to the floor with a loud thud. It didn't break, nor did the perfume bottles. Lori says that was just another way for Dan to tell her, "Hi, I'm okay."

They Did It!

It was a difficult year. Six months after Marianne's mother became ill with lung cancer, Marianne's fifty-year-old sister, Lucy, discovered she had an aggressive brain tumor. Another cancer. Lucy kept the severity of her illness from her mother, not wanting to add to her burden.

Lucy's health deteriorated quickly, so she moved to a nursing home to receive round-the-clock care. Marianne visited her sister daily and read aloud to Lucy from books they both loved. Devastated when Lucy died only six months after her mother, Marianne hoped for a sign that Lucy was doing well.

Emotionally exhausted from the loss of those closest to her, Marianne had a dream that began as a nightmare.

She said, "It began with some teenage thugs pursuing me—a typical bad dream. Then the dream changed. It became

17

very vivid and bright, and suddenly Lucy and my mother appeared, along with my dead father. Dad beat those thugs, who disappeared from the dream along with Dad. Then Mom and Lucy's faces loomed large. Joyfully, they high-fived each other and exclaimed, 'We did it!' They were so delighted that they were able to get through to me. When I woke up, they were both in the room with me. I felt them. And I felt their joy."

Chapter 2
Visitations

Heart talks to heart; soul speaks to soul.

Hazrat Inayat Khan

Visitations occur many different ways. Some souls make themselves felt through our senses—they let us hear, see, smell, or even touch them. Other souls reach out by tapping into our intuitive faculty. And some talented souls have the ability to materialize physically, depending on their skill at manipulating matter from a nonmaterial state. I imagine it's not easy to fashion a body, or more souls would be doing it! Because it's such a rare occurrence, I've designated full embodiment as a separate category. (You'll see that some folks have very creative ways of dematerializing, too!)

A Touching Story

Ceil's story involves visitation through both touch and dreams. When Ceil and her sister were quite young, they took violin lessons from an elderly, gifted woman named Viola. An accomplished musician, Viola loved teaching children, but she was a tough taskmaster. During their lessons, when she didn't like the sounds her students produced, she would firmly press on one of their shoulders. "It hurt," Ceil said, "but it was a clear signal to do better."

They got the message and created purer sounds. Ceil and her sister never mentioned Viola's motivational tactic to their mother, Joan Ellen, because they really liked their teacher and feared that their mom would remove them from her classes. When Viola died suddenly, the whole family was upset; they knew she would be hard to replace.

Many years later, when Ceil was an adult, she talked to Joan Ellen about Viola and what a positive effect she'd had on Ceil's powers of concentration and her musical skills and knowledge. "I was really sad when Viola died," Joan Ellen said. "In fact, one night shortly after her funeral I even dreamed about her, and I awoke to the feeling of someone pressing really hard on my shoulder. It hurt! Somehow I knew it was Viola, but I felt silly telling anyone about it."

"Mom," said Ceil. "Why did you wait twenty years to tell me about this? I wish you had told me this when it happened."

Her mother looked at her quizzically. "Why? I didn't want to frighten you. Besides, I thought you'd think I was crazy! I doubted my own sanity, to tell you the truth."

"Oh, Mom, Viola always pressed us really hard on the shoulder when she wanted to make a point. She was letting you know she was okay." Joan Ellen was relieved to know her experience with Viola was real, and not a product of her imagination gone wild.

Sorry, Wrong Number—Or Not!

Noor-un-Nissa inayat Khan was a very gentle soul who wrote children's stories before World War II. She and her family were pacifists. But when the war broke out and she learned what the Nazis were doing, Noor determined she would do whatever she could to stop them. She became a decoding expert and telegraph operator who developed into one of Britain's top MI-5 agents.

Noor-un-Nissa's story has been told in several books, including William Stevenson's *A Man Called Intrepid* (later made into a Hollywood film celebrating her wartime life and heroic death). I learned from this book that Noor's code name was "Madeleine" and that she was instrumental in helping the Allies defeat the Nazis. In 1944, after being dropped behind enemy lines in France, Madeleine was captured in a farmhouse where she was telegraphing vital information to the British intelligence director, code-named "Intrepid." She could have escaped, but instead she stayed in the farmhouse while others fled because she knew how important it was to send her messages back to England. Her efforts helped turn the tide of the war for the Allies.

After her capture, Madeleine kept escaping from the Germans' minimum-security prisons, and so she was sent to Dachau, where she eventually died. The French government created a plaque commemorating her heroism and installed it on the wall surrounding her ancestral home in Suresnes. A memorial statue honoring her has been erected in London's Gordon Square, as well.

In the late 1970s, immersed in the *Intrepid* book, I felt very inspired by and close to Noor/Madeleine. Her bravery in captivity was quite amazing—she never broke and never divulged any information, although her captors tortured her repeatedly. Years later when they were interviewed, even her torturers remarked on her spiritual power and depth of courage. I read throughout the night to finish the book, finally closing it at nearly 5:00 a.m. I fell asleep thinking about how remarkable she had been. I was jarred awake by the phone's ringing, and I was in a fog as I fumbled for the phone. But I became fully alert when the woman on the line asked in Spanish, "Es Madelaina en tu casa?" *(Is Madeleine in your house?)* Surprised, I replied, "No, ella no está en mi casa." *(No, she is not in my house.)* I hung up the phone, feeling, in fact, that she was "en mi casa"—in spirit, at least. This event was clearly not a wrong number!

Adieu, Dear Friend

Sondra, from Chicago, was visiting New Orleans with her friend Nate when she heard a woman's voice calling her name. They both looked around, but no one was in the street.

"Nate, did you hear what I heard?" Sondra asked.

"Yes," he said. "I heard a woman calling your name, loud and clear."

"It sounded like Sue. I hope she's okay." Sondra's friend Sue, who lived in Indianapolis, had been battling cancer for some time.

Nate and Sondra continued their sightseeing throughout the day and then had dinner. When Sondra returned to her hotel later that evening, she had a message from home: Sue had died that morning. Sondra is certain Sue called out her farewell on her way to the other realm.

Sharon's Loving Visitors

Sharon has experienced several small miracles, including visitations, luminous dreams, and the soul's light touch.

During her husband's illness, Sharon sat daily at his bedside, maintaining her vigil even when he lapsed into a coma. After he was pronounced dead, the nurse left the room so she could have some private time with him. Weeping, she reached for his hand, and she was startled when his dead hand tightly squeezed hers. She also felt a ghostly hand gently touch the calf of her leg. "I never told anyone, not even my son," she said. "It was between my husband and me."

Many months later, Sharon went to a psychic who delivered a message from her husband: "Tell her I squeezed her hand and touched her leg so she'd know I was okay, and to let her know how much she meant to me." Sharon, moved by his message, was relieved to know he was doing well in the afterlife. She says he still comes to visit periodically, giving her loving, feather-light touches on her leg or cheek.

Another beloved family member also communicated with Sharon after his death. When Sharon's dad was alive, he often stopped by and sat on her porch, sharing whatever was on his mind—family matters, the day's events, or politics. Sharon cherished those evenings with her dad, and when he died she missed their chats. One night she had a dream: "He came onto the porch and sat down, just the way he used to, and he said, 'Don't feel bad for me—I'm fine.' The dream was very vivid. I know it was a real communication."

Her husband's feathery touches and her dad's reassuring message have reinforced Sharon's belief that life continues after death.

The Make-A-Wish Boy

Roberta, a volunteer with the Make-A-Wish Foundation, spent several months with four-year-old Timmy, who had been diagnosed with incurable cancer. They became very close during their short time together.

After Timmy died, Roberta visited his mom to pay her condolences and was startled to hear children giggling behind the woman's chair. She discreetly glanced behind the chair, but to her surprise, no one was there. It didn't seem like an appropriate time to mention what she had heard, but many months later she shared the story with Timmy's mom.

"Oh, that was Timmy and his angel friend, Chelsea," the woman said. "Timmy used to tell me she came to visit him often, sometimes sitting at the edge of the bed, sometimes sitting on the dresser—sometimes even hanging from the ceiling! She played with him." Timmy's mom was pleased to hear that they were still laughing and playing together.

A Baby's Cry

When Tara, an old friend, made an unexpected visit to my home, I introduced her to Beth, a visitor whose one-year-old daughter had died several weeks earlier. I invited Tara to join us for tea, but she refused and left rather abruptly. She called later that evening and explained that she had cut her visit short because she kept hearing a baby's cries coming from my bedroom, and she was upset that Beth didn't respond.

"Why did that baby's mother ignore its cries?" she asked. "And why did you ignore it, too? I was so disturbed I had to leave. The poor kid—nobody was paying attention."

"There was no baby in the bedroom," I told her. Then I explained Beth's situation.

"I'm so glad I didn't say anything—I almost did!" Tara said. "That would have been awful for the poor woman to handle."

Was Tara hearing a baby who couldn't leave its mother, or was she telepathically picking up on Beth's sadness? All we know for sure is that she did hear a baby's cry.

The Priest's Story

I heard a classic visitation story from a priest who officiated at the funeral of one of my patients. He described his mother's experience shortly after his father died:

"I spent the first week after the funeral at my mother's home, but then I had to get back to my own parish. The first evening she was alone, Mom said a pounding on her front door awakened her at three o'clock in the morning. Half asleep, she was headed downstairs to answer the door when she heard my newly dead dad say, 'What are you doing? You're an eighty-two-year-old woman opening the door to a total stranger at this hour of the morning—are you crazy? Go back to bed!' That got her attention. She said, 'Thanks, dear—you're still watching out for me.' She went back upstairs while the caller went down the road to a neighbor's house. Mom said she didn't just hear my dad; she felt his presence, too."

After I heard the priest's story, I spoke to him and asked if I could use it.

"Yes," he said. "I want people to be open to possible communications from their loved ones—they will be so comforted. But don't use my name!"

A Cautionary Husband

Mo's story also involves a protective voice from beyond. She shared the story with my grief group, which she joined because she felt isolated and lonely after her husband's death.

"When Tim was alive and well, he handled car repairs, got license plates renewed, mowed the lawn, and handled household tasks," she said. "He was a take-charge kind of guy. When he became gravely ill and couldn't do those things anymore, it really exasperated him, because he felt he was not pulling his weight in our marriage."

"How did you handle it?" another participant asked.

"I took over his jobs willingly—I just wanted him to get well," Mo said. "Believe me, that's all I cared about. I desperately wanted to keep him around. I fed him the right foods and took care of him at home as long as I could. When he entered the hospital and it became clear that he was going downhill, I did all I could to keep him alive. I prayed, I bargained with God, and Tim did stay alive much longer than the doctors predicted. Eventually, though, the cancer got him. We were so in love and well matched—we did everything together. I felt an awful emptiness after he died."

Mo went on to say that her daughter Cassie, who was away at college, worried about her. Although Cassie had her studies to deal with, she called often, came home on weekends, and spent her college vacations at home. But Mo remained depressed.

"One of our favorite trips had been driving up to Michigan to visit Tim's relatives," Mo said. "After Tim died they kept inviting me to come up to visit, but I felt too vulnerable for a long time, so I kept making excuses not to go." Still, she was grateful that they kept trying, and after many months when, once more, her in-laws invited her to spend the weekend with them, she finally felt strong enough to accept.

Mo was packing her suitcase in preparation for the journey when she clearly heard Tim say, "Your car has something wrong with the transmission—it's dangerous to drive that way. Postpone the trip and get it checked out!" She took the car to their trusted mechanic, who discovered that the transmission needed extensive repairs.

Mo later visited Tim's relatives, who welcomed her lovingly, and she was pleased when they invited her to visit again whenever she could get away. "I'm grateful, because the trip helped me break out of my debilitating depression," she said.

Since then, Tim has continued to pull his weight—warning Mo about faulty wiring, reminding her to get her auto license and registration renewed, even prompting her to fix the lawnmower. "I think he's getting a kick out of helping me out from the other side," she said, "because he was so sick the last two years of his life he just couldn't take care of those problems."

Dad the Fixer

Anita's dad, Buddy, was "a mechanical guy" and a frugal one as well. He often came to Anita's home to putter about and repair whatever needed fixing. He knew the intricacies of the wiring in the artificial waterfall and sprinkler system in her yard. She did not, and neither did her husband.

"After my dad's death," she said, "I called a repair company because the waterfall stopped working and the sprinklers wouldn't turn on. The young repairman who arrived couldn't find the electric box that controlled the waterfall, and he said he'd have to destroy the sidewalk to find it. I didn't want the sidewalk destroyed."

After searching the large lawn four times, she said, the young man was getting frustrated. Suddenly all the sprinklers on the far side of the lawn popped up and turned on spontaneously—and neither she nor the repairman was near any electrical outlet. Anita grabbed the metal stick used to turn off the sprinkler system—it stood right next to the patio—and there she found the electric box, embedded in the ground and painted brown to match the patio. Hidden in plain sight!

Anita said, "I'm convinced it was Dad, helping out as usual. The young repairman left, he was so spooked at the spontaneous eruption of half the sprinklers. His boss returned later to complete the job. And the sidewalk stayed intact. I'm glad Dad's still hanging around!"

That Still, Small Voice

Once when my daughter was young, she went with a friend to the skating rink downtown. The friend's mother drove them there, and I was to pick them up. I had left the house and begun driving down William Street when I distinctly heard a voice say, "Don't go William Street, go Elm Street." I argued with it: *Sorry, William Street is shorter.* But again the voice said, "Don't go William Street, go Elm."

The night before, a huge snowstorm had blanketed the streets, leaving the plowed snow piled six or seven feet high on some street corners. Again I heard the warning, and again I ignored it. Then, just as I was crossing a major intersection, a car skidded out of a side street, hit my car broadside, and then slid around and hit it again, completely crumpling the length of the passenger side. My car was totaled.

Fortunately, I was able to crawl out of the driver's side door. My head ached, and I had bruises and a mild concussion but no broken bones. It turned out the teenage driver had stolen his father's car and ignored the stop sign at the intersection where he barreled into my car. Clearly the voice I'd heard was my guardian angel, working overtime to keep me from getting into an accident that was about to happen—or was it my own sharpening intuition? *Or* was it a bit of both: my guardian angel helping to train my intuition? Whatever it was, I could have avoided the collision if only I'd listened to that still, small voice in my head.

Ethereal Visitors

When I was in my twenties, I entered the hospital for a minor surgical procedure. After I awoke from the effects of general anesthesia, a nurse took me to my room where I met my roommate, Agnes, a delightful, friendly woman with beautifully coiffed white hair. We enjoyed conversing on a wide range of topics, and at some point our discussion turned to the afterlife. Agnes, ill and elderly, had dying on her mind, and I was curious about dying, too.

She said, "I'm not too frightened of death, because I can see the souls who've just died floating through the room on their way home. Do you see them, too?"

I thought she was a bit dotty; I didn't see any floating bodies. "No," I replied.

"Well, they're here!" she said empathically. "There they are, see? They're floating across the room."

"No," I said. "I really don't see them."

This isn't unusual—I've heard many similar stories. My own grandmother Rachel saw her long-dead husband often. Sometimes he sat in his favorite chair; other times he'd hover near the ceiling. His presence comforted her, and she was sure he'd be there to greet her when she passed over. I hope he was.

Grandma Rachel also saw angels. When I was younger I thought she was a bit dotty, too. Now, having heard so many stories like hers, I have much more respect for her experiences.

Send Me a Sign, Dad

Bobbie Ann told me that after she lost her dad, a former dentist, she kept asking him to send her a sign that he was happy in the afterlife. Sometime after the funeral, she reached for her phonebook to look up a number and the yellow pages fell open to a large ad for a local dental practice. It featured a huge smiley face. When she saw it smiling up at her, she felt her father's presence and said, "Thanks, Dad!"

After hearing her story I remarked, "He used your intuition to guide you to the right page in the phone book. That's pretty good!"

"That's not the end of it," Bobbie Ann said. "Shortly afterward, the same large yellow smiley face appeared on a billboard that I pass every day to get to work; it just got posted. I nearly drove off the road, laughing, when I felt my father's presence again. It's a daily reminder that Dad's doing just fine. And it is *so* his sense of humor."

The White, Diaphanous Clouds

Arlene, a physician and scientist, describes herself as a "healthy skeptic." However, she has had encounters with both her parents that can't be explained by science. One of them happened right after her seventy-five-year-old dad died unexpectedly from a massive heart attack, and she and her husband, scrambling to make funeral arrangements, were trying to decide between two coffins at the funeral home.

"Both were nice," Arlene said, "but one cost eight hundred dollars more than the other. I kept walking between the two coffins, undecided. I was wearing a lapis necklace my dad had given me many years before, and while I stood in front of the more expensive coffin, the necklace fell off my neck onto the floor. I'm convinced it was my frugal dad's way of saying, 'Not this one, honey!' We bought the cheaper coffin. The necklace had never fallen off my neck before, and it hasn't done it since. That's my dad!"

After the funeral, Arlene, her mother, and her husband were startled to see a white, wispy cloud hovering next to her mother.

Twenty-two years later, as her mother lay dying, Arlene once again saw the diaphanous cloud hovering over the ninety-seven-year-old woman's head. Arlene's husband and their daughter Sylvie were present, too.

"I saw the white cloud, but neither my husband nor my daughter saw it this time," Arlene recalled. "I asked Sylvie to stand where I was standing and take a picture with her phone, aiming it right at my mother's head and the spot above it. The cloud appeared on the photo! After Sylvie e-mailed the photo to me, she was so spooked she took the image off her phone. But I still have it on my desktop—I find it comforting."

"PMA, Wendy, PMA"

Wendy's dad, an optimistic person, was an insurance salesman who truly cared for his clients, tailoring the best possible insurance policy for each client. At his funeral there was an outpouring of sympathy from many whom he had helped. He was well loved by all who knew him, friends and family alike, and he loved his own children unconditionally.

Wendy, who shared his sunny disposition, was very close to her dad. After his death, she often visited his gravesite to talk to him and share what was going on in her life. She followed in his footsteps by going into sales, and because her job required travel, she spent long hours in airports or rental cars.

"My dad always had a way of getting me out of a funk," she said. "If I was unhappy or complaining, he'd say, 'PMA, Wendy, PMA.' Positive Mental Attitude: that was his mantra, and it was how he lived his own life."

One day after her father had been dead for many years, Wendy found herself at an airport with hours to spare because her original flight had been canceled. Restless and grumpy, she decided she'd go to the drugstore down the road, and so, grumbling to herself, she got into her car and left. Entering the Walgreen's parking lot, she parked behind a license plate that read "PMA."

"I laughed," she said. "My dad snapped me out of my bad mood, just like he always did. He guided me to that parking spot and took me from PMS to PMA."

The Stranger's Message

Hours after her husband died unexpectedly of a heart attack, Nora was in her home, grief-stricken and overwhelmed. She had arranged for a funeral home to pick up his body, chosen his wardrobe, picked out a casket, and made funeral arrangements at their church, but she was still in shock. She was standing there in her bathrobe when the doorbell rang. She opened the door to see a somewhat frazzled-looking middle-aged woman wearing mismatched clothes, as if she'd dressed in hurry.

"Do you know a man named Michael?" the woman asked. "I've been sent by him."

Nora said, "My husband's name is—was—Ted Michaelson. He died early this morning."

"Oh," the woman said. "I got it almost right, then. The name came through as Michael. He gave me this address and said, 'Tell my wife I'm okay.'"

Nora, surprised and confused, invited the kind stranger in. But having delivered the message, she declined and left.

When Nora shared her story with me, she began wondering aloud: "Was she a medium of some kind? I have no idea who she was. Was this a one-shot deal for her? I was so surprised I didn't think to ask any questions, but her visit definitely helped me deal with the suddenness of his passing. I'm so grateful he sent her. But how did he do that?"

I didn't have an answer.

The Soul Knows

Sometimes a soul communicates through symbolic actions. Take the case of Mabel, a widow who suffered from severe dementia and, when this story took place, had been nonverbal and uncommunicative for over two years. Carmen was her caregiver, watching over Mabel while her adult children got on with their lives in other cities.

Mabel spent her days roaming the house compulsively and aimlessly, often stopping at the kitchen desk just long enough to write on some sticky notes, and then placing them on the wall wherever the fancy took her. After Mabel fell asleep in the evening, Carmen would retrieve the yellow squares and toss them into the wastebasket. "Otherwise they would have covered the walls, the mirrors, and the stairwell," Carmen explained. "They were everywhere!"

Carmen was with Mabel for a year when she could still talk—"and boy could she talk," Carmen said. "She enjoyed talking about lots of things, and so did I. We became friends. Of course, she got worse, and that ended. That's when she started with the sticky notes. She never did anything with them when she was still aware."

On each sticky note, Mabel would print in large, block letters, JULY 19, 2003. Carmen could not figure out why that date was so important to Mabel—that is, not until Mabel died on July 19, 2003. Somehow, on some very deep level, Mabel knew the date of her own death. And Mabel's soul wanted Carmen to understand that.

"Mabel taught me something special," Carmen said. "She taught me that the soul knows what it knows and will find a way to share its knowledge if it really wants to. I'm grateful to Mabel for being my friend and my teacher."

A Secular Exorcism

I think my friend Larry's tale may be about helping people who are stuck between this world and the next; Larry has other ideas. See what you think …

Soon after Larry and his family moved into a very old house in the Berkshires, he was annoyed to discover that he had "visitors" in one of the upstairs bedrooms. None of his five children would spend time in the room; they were determined not to sleep there because two voices, a male and a female, could often be heard arguing. The creaking of a rocking chair was audible, too.

Larry, a no-nonsense retired military colonel, took steps to rid the house of these ephemeral visitors. He entered the room and said loudly, in his best military voice, "You don't belong here. I bought this house. You have to leave—you don't live here anymore! Go fight somewhere else." The voices abruptly stopped, the rocking chair stopped creaking, and apparently the couple took their argument elsewhere. They were never heard from again.

"I resist using the word 'ghosts' in telling you this story," Larry explained to me. "I think it was just an emotionally charged impression left in the room from some much earlier time."

"I don't know," I said. "Another explanation could be that these were earthbound souls whose negative energies held them in some kind of limbo—that's a kind of ghost. Well, you have your house back, and that's what matters. The negative vibes are gone."

"That's true," Larry said. "We're enjoying the house, and two of the kids now sleep in what used to be a really scary room."

Out of the Mouths of Babes

Children often see their dead relatives, and three-year-old Lesley Ann is a typical example. Her mother, Bunny, was inconsolable after losing her own mother to breast cancer, and sometimes while grieving she wept in front of her small children. One morning Lesley Ann came up to Bunny as she gazed out the living room window.

"Mommy, are you sad because Nonna's gone?" Lesley Ann asked. "Don't cry—look, she's standing there on the sidewalk. She's smiling at us. Don't cry, she's okay, Mommy. She's blowing us kisses." And then the toddler blew kisses back at her grandma.

"I didn't see her, but Lesley Ann surely did," Bunny said later.

And then there was five-year-old Luke, who awoke at three in the morning to tell his parents that Grandpa had appeared on the edge of his bed and told him to "be a good boy, and tell your mom I'm okay. Give her a hug for me." The last Luke's parents knew, Grandpa's leukemia was in remission and he was otherwise healthy. The next morning, however, they learned that Grandpa (who lived in another part of town) had died of a massive heart attack at the same time he visited Luke. Nobody expected it—least of all Luke—but he hugged his mom for Grandpa. She, in turn, was incredibly comforted.

"I'm glad Dad came to Luke," she said. "I probably would have freaked out if he'd come to me!"

Chapter 3

Embodiment: The Materialization of Spirit

Energy is eternal delight.

William Blake

Luke's story is an example of a full embodiment. Children don't have preconceived ideas about soul visits, so loved ones who want to offer information or reassurance can more easily reach them. The following tales relate adult experiences with embodiment, showing that if we stay open to them, such visits can and do happen.

Sara's Double-Digit Caper

We've seen that the river, a metaphor for the soul's final crossing, appears in many myths and legends; the river Styx is only one example of this potent cross-cultural symbol. There are times when people on *this* side of the river have to help those who find it difficult to leave their bodies and let go of earthly life.

Sara, who lives in the Berkshire Hills, often chaperoned her daughter Shana's elementary school field trips. While she was chaperoning a bus tour to Boston, a nasty Florida spider that apparently had come north to visit decided Sara would make a tasty morsel and bit her middle finger. Within a few days, the finger had swollen to dangerous proportions. First doctors lanced the site, and then more drastic surgery was required to save the finger. Upon awakening in the intensive care unit, Sara noticed she was sharing the space with a woman who was hooked up to a life-support system. Although Sara was still woozy from the anesthesia, she was alert enough to see that the elderly woman in the next bed was floating above her own body while still attached to her physical body by her big toe.

"I can't get out," the woman fretted. "I want to leave but I'm stuck. What should I do? I don't want my daughter to be here when I die."

"You're just hanging on by a toe," Sara said. "Wiggle it— that should help."

The woman wiggled her big toe and, sure enough, wrested herself from her earthly body. "Thanks," she said with a smile.

Then, as Sara watched, astonished, the woman's solid hovering body dissolved first into a milky substance and then into a pink mist. Sara's attention was drawn to the life-support hookups; she saw that the woman's vital functions had stopped. Her daughter entered the room with the nurses, but of course it was too late. The old woman had wanted out, so with her roommate's help, she left. Sara took a good look at the body; it looked pretty much like the floating lady, only less animated.

When Sara told me this story, I said she deserved the Cosmic Fickle Finger of Fate Award—and she'd better toe the line, or else!

Great-Uncle Gideon

Rob, an old family friend, was a theater director and teacher before he retired. Rob's great-uncle Gideon "pops in" to visit him periodically. An unpredictable visitor, Gideon has followed Rob from house to house over the years, fully materializing. One particular time, two of Rob's theater students arrived at his home early for an appointment to rehearse lines for a local production. While waiting in the driveway, they were startled to see a man in a top hat and black frock coat walk from the outdoors through the wall of Rob's house and into the living room, where they could see him through the picture window. When Rob arrived, his students told him what they had seen. "Oh, that was just Uncle Gideon making his presence known!" Rob said, but the students were spooked.

Several years later Rob moved into a lovely old Victorian home. Once, when my daughter spent the night there, Gideon appeared in the doorway to her room. The startled teenager covered her head with a blanket and finally fell asleep. Gideon was gone when she awoke. Another time, Rob's friend Terra stopped by for a visit, rang the front doorbell, and watched through the front-door glass as the tall, black-clad, elegant gentleman crossed the foyer, exited the dining room, and entered the living room. Gideon doesn't speak; he just "makes his presence known," as Rob always says. And he's not a ghostly wraith—according to those who've seen him, he's quite solid!

Visiting the Manicurist

When John's young, vibrant wife, Liz, died suddenly, he was devastated. Liz had been a university law professor and a practicing attorney, and, before that, a food critic for a large Midwestern newspaper. Despite the many friends and family members who needed to be told the sad news, the day after Liz's death John felt compelled, somewhat irrationally, to visit the Vietnamese woman who regularly painted her nails. He called her "the nail lady."

"Why the sudden urge?" I asked.

He said, "Liz had gone to this woman for years to get her nails done. I didn't want her to worry when Liz didn't show up for her next appointment, or to think Liz had abandoned her."

When he entered the nail salon holding Liz's photo so he could explain who he was, he discovered the nail lady, Tien, and her husband poring over the front-page newspaper article, apparently just finding out that Liz had died.

The distressed woman told him that Liz had steered them through the process of becoming citizens and advised them on various other legal issues as well. John knew that Liz was an excellent and conscientious attorney, helping and guiding many people of whom she was fond. That apparently included her manicurist.

Tien also told him that Liz had explained the workings of the solar system to her. ("I'd like to have been a fly on the wall to hear that explanation!" John remarked later.)

Then Tien said, "She surprised me last night—she came and sat on the edge of my bed. I saw her from the corner of my eye. She held my hand and said, 'Don't worry, I am fine. I am okay. And you'll be okay, too. Don't worry.' But when I turned my head to get a better look at her, she disappeared!'" At that point, Tien didn't know of Liz's passing.

John told me he was surprised and relieved to hear that Liz was okay. I remarked that she had reached John through his intuition, guiding him to visit Tien so she could deliver the message. He was clearly too deep in his own grief for Liz to appear to him directly.

"Well, I don't know about that, Bonney," John said. "I'm just giving you the facts."

I commented that Tien's ancient culture is probably more accepting of soul appearances than our own, in which fear essentially blocks such communication.

Brother Moe Comes to Play

Early on in Mick and Tammy Jo's first pregnancy, they named their baby boy (they were sure it was a boy) Michael Jr. Unfortunately, the pregnancy ended in a full-term miscarriage, and the expectant parents were devastated at the loss. The distraught couple decided to name the dead baby "Moe" rather than the name they had originally chosen. Several years later, they had a daughter, Susie. When Susie was almost three years old, she said, "Mommy, I know my brother Joe. He came to say hello. He's a nice boy."

Tammy Jo said she and Mick had never discussed the earlier pregnancy with Susie. "We were surprised enough that our daughter knew she had a brother," she said. "But the name is so close—Joe sounds enough like Moe, and my name is Tammy Jo—that it is unlikely Susie plucked it out of the ether. When we asked her about it again, Susie insisted that her brother had come to see her and that they had had fun. Mick and I feel Moe wanted to meet his sister and to let us know he feels our love as well."

Three Wise Women

In life, Don and his mom were close, and they stayed that way after she died: she occasionally "checked in" with Don, emitting light and love. She appeared to him first as a felt presence; eventually he could actually see her as a shimmering presence from the corner of his eye.

One day he felt her near, but he also sensed two other strong female presences. Surprised and delighted, he watched them fully materialize. The veil between the worlds had completely lifted: he saw his mother standing next to his aunt and his grandmother. They were joyous, infused with and surrounded by light. "They were grinning at me," he recalled. "They were so happy being together, and they wanted me to know it."

Don is a doctor who possesses a strong intuitive faculty as well as a strong scientific side, so he was interested in observing the progression of his mother's spirit from felt sense to peripheral vision to full materialization. "I loved seeing those three special women, but the scientist in me also loved observing how the vision unfolded. What a rich experience!"

Moving through the Tunnel

Don was also close to his stepdad, Fred, who had helped raise him from the time he was a toddler. When Don was in high school, his mom divorced Fred, and Don lost touch with him. Fred eventually remarried and moved to another state.

Don was in his fifties when he heard Fred was gravely ill. He traveled a long distance to visit Fred and thank him for being such a good, loving dad through Don's crucial childhood years; afterward they stayed in touch by phone until Fred died. Several weeks later, Fred materialized in Don's room, apparently confused and unaware that he was dead. Don helped guide him to the other side simply by discussing everyday things.

"How are the children? How's Louise?" Don asked. "And how are you doing?"

"Okay, I guess," Fred replied. "But I don't know where I am or what to do next."

Don saw a small, bright white light. "Just move around, Fred. Do you see the light?"

"No."

"Well, move around a bit more. Do you see it now?"

"Yes, a bit."

"Move toward it, Fred."

"It's getting brighter."

"Turn again, Fred."

Each time Fred turned, the light not only intensified, but it also enlarged, opening into a tunnel leading to other dimensions.

"Move through the tunnel," Don advised.

Fred did so, saying, "It's so bright ... so beautiful!" Excitedly, he skipped through the tunnel. Don watched Fred enter the tunnel. As he exited from the right, a long arm reached out from the tunnel's left side and waved at Don.

"I don't know who waved," he said, "but it surprised me. Life is full of surprises!"

And so it is!

Materializing Mike

Michael was born with multiple sclerosis and spent most of his life in a wheelchair. Susan and Joanne, who were sisters, knew Michael for many years; Susan, his closest friend, always said she loved his wicked sense of humor. When he was in his forties, his health began to fail, and he told the women that when he crossed over, he'd use electricity to let them know he was fine.

Not long afterward Michael died, and after the funeral the women returned to their separate homes. Susan entered the front door and flipped on the light—and the whole house's electricity shut down. She tripped the master switch in the basement and then phoned Joanne. But before she could share her story, Joanne said, "Guess what? I came home, turned on the light, and blew the master circuit. All the house lights went off!"

"He did it to me, too!" Susan said. "He must be okay!"

The sisters told me about Michael while we sat vigil at their dying mother's bedside. I said, "That's a great story. Can I use it?"

"Sure," Susan said, "but that's not the end of the story. The very next day, Michael appeared in my dining room doorway, smiling—still in his wheelchair but otherwise looking very healthy. And he said, 'Dying is so easy. One breath on the earth and the next breath on the other side. I'm fine. Tell Joanne.'"

"Did he look like a ghost? Was he transparent?" I asked.

"No, he was as solid as you are," she replied. "But he disappeared right after that—just winked out!"

Joanne said, "We know Mom will be okay, too, because of Michael."

A Heaven-Sent Messenger

Jim, a participant in my grief group, told us the following story while seated beside his forty-year-old daughter, Sandy:

"When Sandy was eleven years old she was diagnosed with a vicious, invasive cancer. The doctors were doing their best to save her life, but it was touch and go. Months of treatments, ranging from chemotherapy to surgery, left her in a very weakened condition. My wife and I were grief-stricken—we were terrified of losing our child. We are devout Catholics, so every day I spent time in the hospital chapel praying to God that He would save my child.

"I was alone in the chapel one day, deeply focused in prayer, when I felt a tap on my shoulder. It startled me, and I turned to see a black nurse in a white uniform. She looked me straight in the eye and said, 'Don't worry, your daughter will recover. She's going to be okay.' Tears filled my eyes, so I blinked—and the nurse disappeared. In the blink of an eye."

"Wow," I said. "Angels come in many guises."

"That was no angel," Jim said, pointing a finger emphatically at me, "that was God. I was praying to God. I didn't know God was a black nurse!"

Jim and his daughter, long ago cured of the cancer that had invaded her body, sat side by side, relishing the story. Sandy had regularly attended the grief group since her mother died of cancer months before; concerned for her grieving father, she asked him to attend the group so he could express his feelings. A very private person, Jim withdrew after attending several sessions. I hope sharing his pain helped him move forward; his wise, insightful contributions helped other group members understand their own issues.

Chapter 4

Manipulating Matter

There are more things in heaven and earth, Horatio, than are dreamt of in your philosophy.

William Shakespeare

Manipulating matter is another way people connect with their earthly relatives and friends through creative play. Examples of this sort of interaction are fairly plentiful, so I've somewhat arbitrarily created a separate category for those stories, although they certainly could also be described as soul visitations. The following stories show a wide range of attention-getting devices. My mother is a master matter manipulator, so I'll start out with a story about her.

Happy Birthday, Dear Daughter

Since the death of my mother, Minnie, in 1969, my continuing relationship with her has developed against a backdrop of joyous playfulness.

Minnie was born in Russia in 1917, one of my grandparents' younger children. My grandfather, a brilliant, legally trained civil servant, was invited by the Bolsheviks to retain his position after the revolution, provided he abandon his Jewish religion. He refused, deciding instead to leave Russia with his wife and five children— not an easy task, considering that they had to flee by night and hide by day. After living in several European countries during a difficult, traumatic four-year period, they boarded a boat to the United States. Along the way the three youngest children contracted measles; one of the girls died. Minnie survived but was temporarily blind during what must have been a disorienting and frightening boat trip to America. She was five years old at the time.

When they arrived in the United States in 1922, Minnie's parents couldn't remember her birth date. (She was one of three daughters born within three years, so the confusion was understandable.) When Minnie learned to read, her mother told her to choose a birthday from the "American" calendar between Hanukkah and Christmas; the Russian calendar was quite different, so the dates were approximate.

Minnie chose December 9. Coincidentally, I was born on her eighteenth birthday.

After her death, Minnie continued to "pop in" on or around our birthday. Her presence was so obvious it became a family joke. Once, my daughter Lori and I were driving through the Berkshires, chuckling about the many Minnie coincidences, when a Winnebago cut in front of us. It was too close for comfort, and I leaned on the horn—and then we noticed, hand-painted on the rear door in beautiful calligraphy, the words *Minnie's Winni*. Hello from Minnie, once again.

Another time my friend Tryshe and I were driving the 150 miles from the Berkshires to Malden, Massachusetts, to pick up my Aunt Ency, Minnie's youngest sister. Ency and her husband owned the dry cleaning plant where Minnie had worked until her death years before. Tryshe and I discussed many things during the three-hour trip. Inevitably, since it was close to December 9, we wondered how Minnie would celebrate our joint birthday.

"Listen, Mom," I said aloud, "what I really need is a new fur coat. Mine's falling apart and it's *cold* in the Berkshires." I'd bought the coat I was wearing years ago, in a second-hand shop in New York, and it had served me well, considering it had cost all of fifty dollars. But now the fur was falling out in clumps and was about to die a second death.

After Tryshe and I had a good laugh over the coat, we talked of men, life, love, joy, despair, lousy choices—you get the picture. When we arrived at the Malden store, Ency was closing up shop.

"Bonney," she said, "go down to the basement. There's a bunch of fur coats against the back wall that now belong to us since they've been unclaimed for over eight years. Pick one out for yourself. I'll give the rest to charity."

"Coat?" Tryshe giggled as she accompanied me downstairs. I reached into the pile and grabbed a mink coat, vintage 1940s. It was in really good shape and fit me perfectly. I brought it upstairs.

"Oh," Ency said. "That's a nice coat. Let's check to see how long it's been here."

She sifted through the yearly tickets that were stapled together on the sleeve. When she found the intake ticket, it was marked in my mother's distinctive handwriting: *Minnie, 1968, Fur Storage.* Wasn't that a lovely gift from a loving mother?

Just before a recent birthday, Minnie appeared to me in a dream. "Wake up!" she demanded. "There's something for you on the TV."

Ever the dutiful daughter, I awoke and checked the clock. Good grief—it was 4:30 a.m.! But knowing better than to try to go back to sleep, I went into the living room and switched on the TV. It happened to be tuned to channel 9, which was playing a *very* old cartoon set to the music of Cab Calloway singing "Minnie the Moocher." Honest! The visuals were even funnier. Skeletons and ghostly cartoon characters rose wraithlike from their graves in a cemetery filled with singing and dancing creatures. They looked like the holographic ghosts in Disneyland. This gift wasn't as tangible as the mink, but it was certainly just as much fun. "Hi-dee-hi-dee-ho!" (For those youngsters among you, these are part of the clever lyrics of "Minnie the Moocher.")

Here's another bit of synchronicity: just as I was typing the above story, I heard the radio announcer say that the music I'd been listening to was Franz Lizt's "Totentanz" (or "The Dance of Death") and Richard Strauss' "Death and Transfiguration." Isn't life interesting—and isn't death? And isn't Minnie good at cross-temporal communication? She's got a master's degree in manipulating matter.

I don't mean to give the impression that fun is the only focus of the universe. Clearly, pain and destruction are part of the cosmic outpouring. We can see it in the birth and death of stars and galaxies. Galaxies and planets collide; they aren't always orderly. And, as Buddha said, all sentient beings experience pain. Certainly we all do. But we also have the capacity to experience joy. Indeed, how would we recognize joy if we hadn't known pain? What most spiritual disciplines teach is that there are various tasks we must perform at all levels of existence. When you love your work, earthly or heavenly, life (or life *beyond* life) is much more joyful, and full of creative opportunities.

M Is for Miracles

Mary was more than a younger sister to Eleanor: she was Eleanor's best friend and confidante, a woman Eleanor deeply respected for her integrity. When Mary died, Eleanor was overcome with grief.

Eleanor said, "I know everyone feels their departed loved ones are special, but Mary truly was a very unique person. After she died I suffered her loss each and every day. Some days were worse than others. I couldn't focus or concentrate on my family or my work."

On one particularly bad morning six months after her sister's death, Eleanor awoke from an almost sleepless night of tossing, turning, and crying about her loss. As she was lying in bed, she asked Mary, "Is there really more, is there really something after death?" Upon arising she opened the shades and saw that it had snowed heavily the night before—and on her front lawn, written in the newly fallen snow, was an elegant, eight-foot-tall letter *M*.

"It was early morning," Eleanor said later. "Not a soul was out. No one. There were no footprints leading to or away from the large *M*. It was perfectly formed in the deep snow. I relaxed and slept soundly after Mary responded to my plea. Mary helped me begin to heal. How did she do this? Only Mary knows. She must be a wise old soul."

Send Us a Sign, Dad

Robert, his brother, and several cousins were in the funeral home at his father's wake. The men stood at the casket, quietly reminiscing about the deceased. Each man said his private good-byes, both spoken and silent, before the chapel doors were to be opened for other mourners to enter.

Robert, sensing his dad's presence and wanting to know he was okay, said aloud, "Give us a sign that you're all right, Dad."

The air in the room was perfectly still. Suddenly one of several large bouquets near the casket began moving vigorously, as if two unseen hands were forcefully shaking it. The startled men looked at each other and broke out into laughter.

Robert said, "Okay, Dad, we know you're here."

When Robert told me the story later, I asked, "How did your brother react?"

"My brother kind of freaked out in a good way," Robert replied, "and he said, 'Why does this kind of thing only happen when you're around?' I said, 'Maybe it's because I'm open to these experiences.'

"It was a typical Dad move—definitely in character! And I got my sign. Dad was doing just fine. During the second day of the wake, I could see him in a wispy form, moving around the room. When people he cared for approached the casket to view the body, Dad became more visible and more animated. Like when his friend Dotty appeared, his spirit seemed to surround her and comfort her.

"When he was alive, my Dad was reserved emotionally, but once he dropped his body he became much less reserved. He came to me in dreams for some months afterward, surrounded by light, and helped me move toward the next stage in my life."

How Long Is a Week in Heaven?

When Mel's mom, Rhonda, died after a prolonged illness, his dad, George, who was also gravely ill, reported that Rhonda's spirit had visited him in his hospital room, saying, "Don't worry, I'll be there with you for the first week."

George was comforted by her words. "Don't worry about me," he told Mel, smiling. "I'll be fine when I go. Mom's going to take care of me—at least for the first week." George died shortly afterward.

After George's funeral, Mel and his wife, Aggie, began packing up George's possessions. One of the items they had to cope with was his computer, which was still turned on in his den. Although the computer had come equipped with a fax program, George, a technophobe, had never used it. He'd never even hooked up to a phone line. "My dad used the computer the way you'd use a typewriter," Mel explained. "He just didn't have to return the carriage."

While the couple was deciding what to do with the computer, the fax program suddenly launched, and in the middle of the screen where the messages would normally appear, the word *GEORGE* showed up in large, bright-yellow letters. It turns out that George was better at computer usage after his death than while he was alive—apparently he'd kept on learning. Aggie and Mel felt that George's fax message indicated he had successfully made the transition to the other side.

Aggie said, "We assume that Rhonda spent the 'first week' with him, as promised, and got him acclimated to the new reality. How long is a week in heaven, anyway?"

Ellen's Family Ties

When my friend Ellen was fifteen, she shared a bedroom with her sixteen-year-old sister, Jen. That year Jen stepped off the sidewalk one day and was killed by a bus. Ellen was devastated. Their mother had died when the girls were very young, and now losing her sister as well understandably plunged Ellen into grief. The evening of Jen's funeral, after the visitors left, Ellen went to their shared bedroom and cried herself to sleep. She awoke in the night to hear her sister breathing and even tossing and turning in bed, just as she had when she was alive. Knowing she was not alone comforted Ellen. "Jen's nightly visits continued until the bed was dismantled and removed from the room," she said. "I am so grateful to my sister for gracing me with her presence and helping me get through that horrible time."

Ellen's dad was a heavy smoker who never gave up the habit even after he was diagnosed with lung cancer. She took loving care of her father during his illness, and he often told me, his informal chaplain, how much he loved and appreciated her. When Ellen couldn't be there, she arranged for shift nurses to take care of her dad at home. The nurses reported that he would turn off his oxygen, open the window, and have a cigarette or two, even as he was dying. When he entered the hospital in the final stages of his illness, he had to stop smoking. That didn't make him happy!

"Since his death," Ellen says, "he's been stopping by every now and then. He makes his presence known by filling the air with the smell of cigarette smoke."

Although Ellen is not a smoker herself, she is both comforted and amused by his visits. Her father clearly has retained his sense of humor.

With no actual family left, Ellen has forged strong friendships with people who've become her extended family. Still, her blood relatives have sustained her— first her sister, when she was a teen, and then her Dad, who continues to check in.

Getting Samantha's Attention

Apparently, some folks tend to be on the receiving end of peculiar methods of contact by those who have just crossed over. At least that's the case with Samantha, a certified nursing assistant who is especially prone to *loud* noises when she's being reached. Her deceased patients seem to know this.

"My patients know how to get my attention," she says. "It happens fairly often with those I've cared for over a long period of time, or others I've gotten really close to over a short period of time. The important ingredient is that we have bonded." Nursing assistants are an important part of a hospice team. Because they bathe and feed patients, they become very close to them. Those patients who are able to communicate often call nursing assistants their "angels," and families look forward to their visits.

Samantha lives alone, in an unattached house. There are no close neighbors sharing a wall to account for the following events.

One evening, while Samantha was watching TV, she heard what sounded like a hand knocking loudly against the wall in the hallway. She investigated; the banging continued. Afraid someone had entered her home, she phoned her next-door neighbor. He came over and they checked the whole house together, but they found no broken windows or unlocked doors. The next day, Samantha discovered that one of her favorite patients, Doreen, had died an hour before Samantha heard the pounding. Doreen was crazy about Samantha (she called Samantha her "girlfriend"), and Samantha felt the pounding was Doreen's way of saying good-bye. She based this theory on several similar incidents that had happened to her.

For example, early one morning Samantha was startled from a sound sleep when her dresser drawer opened and then slammed shut, loudly and emphatically. The next morning, Samantha discovered that her longtime patient Marta had expired at about the same time the slamming occurred. In fact, Samantha said she felt Marta's presence in the room—she, too, had come to say good-bye.

Before doing hospice work, Samantha had worked in a hospital where she and one of her patients, Joe, had established a close connection. She wasn't present when he died, but she said that when she felt his "breath" passing her cheek, she knew he was gone. Although she wanted to attend his funeral, she was given the wrong date and so she missed the service, which she thought was on Friday. Late on Thursday, the night of his actual funeral, she awoke to the sound of a loud bang coming from her bedroom closet. She didn't figure out what it was until she discovered she had inadvertently missed the funeral. It was Joe saying, "Where were you?"

"Noises are their specialty with me," Samantha said. "I'm used to it now."

Let It Snow, Let It Snow

During a sad late-autumn trip to attend his grandson's funeral in Chapel Hill, North Carolina, Mario reminisced about Joshua, who had loved snow as a child. Whenever Joshua visited his grandparents Mario and Sandra in the Berkshire Hills, where it snows profusely, he'd roll in the snow, often without wearing a coat. His exuberance extended into his young adulthood. Unfortunately, there was darkness in Joshua's life, too. He battled depression and didn't respond well to conventional treatments. Finally, at age twenty-eight, he devastated the family by committing suicide.

As Mario and Sandra drove from Massachusetts to Chapel Hill, they were surprised when it began to snow heavily. Heavy snow is not common in Chapel Hill at that time of year. "That was Josh saying hello," Mario said. "He really loved that snow."

Sandra and Mario attended the funeral. It was, of course, extremely difficult for the whole family. It's out of the order of things for a young man to precede his parents and grandparents in death.

On the return trip home, Sandra and Mario once again shared memories of Joshua, lapsing into silence as they thought about their beloved grandson. "I prayed he was in a peaceful place, and I hoped for a sign," Mario said. "I just wanted to know he was finally at peace. Then a car passed ours, and the license plate was imprinted with JOSHUA. I was so relieved. I said to Sandra, 'That's Josh's way of saying he's okay.'"

She agreed. "Wow. He's pretty good at that for someone who's just crossed over."

Hugs and Holy Carnations

Margarite is a nurse whose considerable healing skills are matched only by her loving compassion. Margarite's mother was a large, loving woman. She was a hugger.

"When my mother hugged me, I felt enveloped in her arms," Margarite recalled. It was such a joy being hugged by her. One morning after her death I dreamed she was holding me in one of her bear hugs … it was so real. When I awoke, I still felt her hugging me, and her presence was palpable. I felt her arms around me."

When Margarite's father-in-law, Papa Joe, died, his sister Marie, an Alzheimer's patient, had been comatose for over a year. Marie died shortly after Papa Joe's passing. When she heard about Marie's death, Margarite remarked to a friend, "Papa Joe died first so he could be there to help Marie over to the other side." As she spoke, she felt his presence, and suddenly there was a strong scent of carnations in the room. It was December, and there were no flowers in the house or garden. Margarite says, "That was Papa Joe's way of saying 'Yes, I did die first so I could help Marie make the transition.'" The nose knows.

Blessings from the Beloved

Here's another example of spirits who are good at manipulating matter. My friend Qahira was raised in a family that openly acknowledged the mysticism and joy of embodying the spiritual dimension in everyday life. Her father, Fatha, was at one time the personal secretary to Hazrat Inayat Khan, who brought the Sufi message to the western world in the 1920s. Qahira often spoke of her extraordinary parents, who had been dead for many years by the time I met her.

I used to travel to California on business, and when I did I often visited Qahira and her family in Camarillo. They lived in a small house with several retreat huts on their property, as well as a cabin that had belonged to her mother, Murshida Bhakti. Given a choice of sleeping spaces, I always chose her mother's cozy cabin. Murshida Bhakti's objects still filled the space, and it was clear to me that she and I shared a quirky sense of humor. I love wordplay, and so did she: on one wall hung a round plate inscribed with the words *A Round Tuit*. I noticed that we shared not only many of the same interests, but also some of the same books on spirituality, religion, mysticism, and psychology.

The cabin's walls and shelves held family photographs, including several of Fatha. He was incredibly handsome, and to the degree that one can have a crush on someone long dead, I was smitten. (Or was I smote?) I fantasized about what it would have been like had we met, and I certainly understood why Murshida Bhakti fell in love with him. He was so magnetic, so charming, so handsome … *Why don't they make men like that today?* I lamented.

I could also see why he fell in love with Murshida Bhakti. She was intelligent, attractive, and, even in her photographs, charismatic. Qahira had told me stories about their romance and their subsequent life together. Because Fatha traveled the globe for his work, the family experienced long separations. And Fatha was fairly young when he died; Murshida Bhakti lived much longer than her husband.

Outside her cabin she had planted a lovely rose garden. Once, while sitting there amid her flowers, I mused about these two special people who had parented my beloved friend, and I felt Murshida Bhakti's loving presence. I closed my eyes, "saw" her welcoming me to her garden, and felt lovingly blessed.

After the trip, I returned home to Chicago. My daughter Lori stopped by and asked how Qahira and her family were doing. I described my "meeting" with Murshida Bhakti in her rose garden, and I told Lori about my crush on Fatha, admitting I wished I could meet someone like him in the flesh! Because it was an unseasonably warm December day, Lori and I decided to take a walk by the lake. We laughed as the wind whipped up; we talked about the wind being the embodiment of the Holy Spirit.

We ambled along, becoming so engrossed in conversation that we didn't take our usual route, and we found ourselves on a road between the park and the lake. As we walked we discussed the fact that whoever wrote the Christmas carol about "angels bending near the earth" really understood the metaphysical truth that at this time of year, near the winter solstice, the veil between this world and the next is much thinner, and disembodied friends, guides, and angels can reach us more easily through intuition, dreams, and visitation.

Then our conversation returned to Fatha—at which point we came upon a yellow Volkswagen with a license plate frame imprinted with the words *Barakat Bashad*.

"What do you think that means?" Lori asked. Looking more closely, we discovered a translation underneath the plate: "Blessings from the Beloved." Certainly, we joked, that was a message from angels bending near the earth. Then imagine our astonishment when the *next* car, a shiny new white Cadillac with maroon upholstery, had a license plate with big bold letters for all the world to see: FATHA.

"Blessings from the Beloved," indeed. I'd still like to meet someone like him in the flesh!

Chapter 5

Letting Go/Crossing Over

To die will be an awfully big adventure.

Sir J. M. Barrie, Peter Pan

The concern of many patients and families is how and when they will cross over. Some dying patients resist letting go; others are anxious to cross over and move through the veil separating the physical and nonphysical worlds. Most of the following stories involve disembodied visitors, but the main focus of these tales is making the crossing.

The River of No Return

In 1958, while my husband, Dick, and I lived in Albuquerque during his military service, we befriended another young couple, the Coxes. We were the typical young, uprooted service family—living away from home for the first time, with very small children. Like Dick, Bob Cox was an air force lieutenant, and Anne Cox and I became quite close. Our families separated when Dick's military service was completed and we returned with our daughter to the East Coast.

Although Anne and I wrote infrequently, we continued to exchange long Christmas letters. Then, just before one Christmas, I had a series of disturbing dreams about Anne. In my dreams, she stood across a narrow river, dressed in her favorite green toreador pants and white ruffled blouse. (Anne was a striking blonde who looked terrific in green.) The surrounding landscape was also a lush green, and full of bright sunlight. The conversation varied from dream to dream, but the gist of it was:

Anne: "Bonney, I'm lost. I need to talk to you. I don't know where I am."

Bonney: "Well, then, come over here. It's not far. Jump across the river—it's not very wide."

Anne: "I can't. I have to stay here."

Bonney: "Then I'll come over there."

Anne: "You can't. You don't belong here yet. You have to stay on your side of the river."

I would awaken puzzled. What did she mean? I mailed her a Christmas card asking what was wrong. She seemed more agitated with each dream, and I worried when I didn't receive her annual card in return. Finally, long after Christmas, I received Bob's letter describing the tragic accident that took place on a high hill near Taos, New Mexico, where Anne and her mother were returning from a shopping trip. Their car was rounding a curve when a car piloted by a drunken driver struck it head-on. Both cars plunged to total destruction far below.

I was, of course, distraught by the news of Anne's death. But at least the letter clarified her bewilderment in my dreams. She was already dead when I began dreaming about her. She'd been raised to believe in a traditional "heaven" ... maybe she'd found herself in an unfamiliar landscape that didn't fit her expectations.

I didn't quite understand how to help her; I was very young. But I intuited that meditating on her eternal soul surrounded by light would be helpful, so that's what I did. I felt better after the meditation—and the disturbing dreams stopped. I hoped the meditation helped her as much as it did me, but of course I had no way of knowing if, or how, her confusion had cleared up.

I was touched that Anne chose to appear to me. She hardly looked wraithlike—in fact, she looked wonderfully healthy, and not at all dead. I was comforted by the fact that her attempts to contact me began *after* the accident. She'd clearly survived death with enough of her personal consciousness intact that she chose to dress up for the occasion. And in her favorite outfit, at that!

There is a sequel to this story. More than twenty years later, I was on a camping trip to New Mexico with two friends and we stopped in Taos. It was my first time there. As we left town, we found ourselves on a steep, winding road high above a breathtakingly beautiful valley. Suddenly Anne's presence was palpable. I closed my eyes and saw her with my inner vision, as if I were watching a movie in my mind. I hadn't thought of Anne in years, yet there she was: smiling, happy, no longer bewildered.

"This is where I crossed the river," she said.

I was delighted to know she was happy and, clearly, no longer bewildered. For me, more than twenty years had passed; for Anne, existing beyond time and space, it could have felt like just the blink of an eye. She was still dressed in her favorite green toreador pants and white ruffled blouse.

Wait for Me, Dad

Ronnie's dad was chronically ill, but his death was not imminent. One night when Ronnie was in that space between sleeping and waking, he felt his father's presence in the room. He opened his eyes, saw his father's face before him, and knew something was wrong. Just as he rose from his bed, he heard the phone ring—it was his sister calling to say his dad was declining. Ronnie dressed hurriedly and headed for his father's home.

Please, Dad, don't die, he thought. *Wait for me.*

When Ronnie arrived, his dad was in a coma. The family surrounded him, said their final farewells, and let him know it was okay for him to leave. At that point he opened his eyes, stared straight into Ronnie's eyes, and died.

"I knew he waited for me," Ronnie said. "That glance said it all. I'm so glad he heard my prayer."

It doesn't take much consciousness or energy to keep the body running; it's like an idling car that requires a small amount of gasoline to keep going. So in that low-key state, the soul can wander about a bit, as Ronnie's dad did, and visit loved ones. If you are open and sensitive, you will know if you've been visited.

Sometimes when a soul has difficulty letting go of the body, it may do so in stages, particularly if a person has emotionally based "unfinished business." When that happens, family members can help ease the transition by giving permission for leave-taking. Simply saying, "It's okay for you to leave, Grandpa. We love you, and we don't want you to be in pain anymore," will help the patient cross the bridge into the next life.

The Power of Music

Maxine cared for her ailing husband, Edwin, for many years, but eventually he became so debilitated he had to be moved to a nursing home. At first he resisted, but he finally reconciled himself to the place, understanding that Maxine, herself frail, could no longer care for him at home. She used classical music—something Edwin loved—to ease the transition. As his body wasted away from a rare neurological disorder, music soothed his mind and spirit.

When Edwin was younger, he and Maxine attended many concerts and Fourth of July celebrations featuring his favorite piece, Beethoven's Ninth Symphony. But his fifteen-year-long illness presented a logistical challenge to him and his caregiver wife, and so when he was no longer able to attend concerts, Maxine played the symphony for him on a CD player in their home and eventually on an iPod in the nursing home.

During the final months of Edwin's illness, he would argue with his long-dead mother, who kept telling him to "come home." She appeared to him in a corner of the room, and she was very persuasive, but he—in a very logical and lawyerlike fashion—kept telling her he wasn't yet ready to leave Maxine. "Please, Mother, be patient," he said. "I need more time."

At the end of his illness, Maxine played his beloved classical music every day for him in his room in the nursing home. Unable to speak, he shared his joy with his eyes and in small gestures.

"I'd lie on the bed with him, listening to Beethoven," Maxine said. "One particular day, when Beethoven was finished, I felt moved to sing 'Over the Rainbow' for him. Then I left, planning to return after he'd been fed his dinner—it was his favorite, ravioli. When I arrived home, the nurse called me to say that he was rapidly declining and I should return as soon as possible. I got into the car and sped back to the nursing home, but he died while I was en route. He clearly didn't want me to be present when he passed; he knew it would be too hard for me. So after his delicious meal, he left."

Maxine believes "Over the Rainbow" created a bridge that eased his way for crossing over to the other side, where he finally joined his mother. Maxine, who loved Edwin's mom, said, "He was in very good hands."

"Over the Rainbow" … Again

Gloria's grandmother Emma, a longtime nursing home patient, began to decline rapidly. For several weeks before the end, she kept seeing her husband and daughter, both of whom had died years before. She'd often converse with them as they encouraged her to come with them.

When Emma's living daughter, Eva, came to visit, she would play a selection of her mother's favorite songs on an iPod. The iPod was set on "shuffle," meaning the songs played in no particular order. Among them were two songs Emma and her husband had shared throughout their long marriage: "Spanish Eyes" and "Over the Rainbow."

One day shortly before Emma died, her dead husband and daughter appeared. Emma turned to Eva, who was sitting at her bedside. "They're hugging each other," she whispered.

"I couldn't see them," Eva recalled later, "but Mom clearly could. Her eyes were wide open, bright and shining."

"Spanish Eyes" played on the iPod, and Emma listened to the whole song. As it ended, she smiled, and a single tear rolled down her cheek; then, while listening to the opening strains of "Over the Rainbow," she took her last breath. And once again, a rainbow bridge helped someone make the crossing.

A short time after the funeral, Gloria and several other family members were at a local McDonald's, sharing Grandma Emma stories, when "Spanish Eyes" played on the sound system. They felt Emma's presence. "She was joyfully saying hi to us and checking on her great-grandkids," said Gloria.

A Grandfather's Decision

Tony and Carmella were sweethearts whose love never dimmed throughout their long married life. After Carmella died, the elderly Tony—a sweet, courtly Italian gentleman—moved in with his daughter, Emilia, and her family. On the first anniversary of his wife's death he entered the dining room in his gray, pinstriped "going-to-church" suit, complete with boutonniere.

"Pa," Emilia said. "Why are you wearing your good clothes? It's not Sunday."

"Well," he announced, "I've discharged my obligation to your mother: I've mourned her for a full year. Tonight I'm going to join her—I'm ready. And she's waiting for me."

The grandchildren giggled, and Emilia smiled. "Sure, Pa. You're as healthy as a horse! Why don't you wait a while?"

Tony just finished his meal and said, "I'm going upstairs to take a nap. It was a great meal, as usual. *Molto bella!* Thank you. You've been a great daughter."

He kissed the grandchildren, climbed the stairs, and lay down on his bed, still decked out in his favorite suit. Emilia discovered him a few hours later with his hands folded across his chest and a beatific smile on his face. As promised, he died peacefully in his sleep, leaving his earthly body and rejoining his beloved sweetheart.

Family Reunion

Fran attended my grief group because she was still having difficulty coping after her husband's death more than a year earlier. She was a mature woman who helped others in the group deal with their emotional pain, even though hers was still very raw, too. Her husband, Luke, had suffered from cancer, and the disease had progressed slowly and painfully. When Fran could no longer care for him herself, he entered a nursing home, and as the illness progressed he went into hospice care.

"Luke and I had such a good relationship—a real love match," Fran said. "It was hard letting him go, and just as hard for him to leave me. I helped raise his kids from his first marriage—his daughter, the eldest, never fully accepted me. We still try. But his son is like my own. And I have the grandchildren. They are a comfort."

Luke lingered for quite some time in hospice care; his pain was somewhat controlled, so he held on to life because he worried about leaving Fran alone. He refused his full complement of painkillers to remain conscious for Fran, who visited him every night after work. She was distressed that he was in pain, and she prayed for a peaceful passing.

The last week before he entered a coma, Luke kept insisting that his sister Dot and his brother Mike were standing nearby, waiting for him.

Fran said gently, "Luke, they both died last year."

He gestured toward the wall and said, "I know. But there they are!"

Just before he died, Luke awoke from his coma. He opened his eyes, gripped Fran's hand and said, "I'm fine. Dot and Mike are here with me. They're in healthy bodies. But I'm really worried about you. Will you be okay?"

Fran was deeply touched by his concern. "Yes," she said.

"I love you," Luke said. Then he closed his eyes, sank back into a coma, and died. Fran is convinced the three siblings were reunited. And the group work has helped. She's doing better and moving on.

A Medieval Home

Arthur and I taught at the same community college. He was a physically fit physics professor who rode his bike to and from work every day. One rainy morning, his bike skidded and he fell off and cracked his head on the curb, losing consciousness. It was a life-threatening injury, and he was rushed to the hospital. As emergency medical technicians tried unsuccessfully to revive him, Arthur had what he later recognized as an out-of-body experience. He was walking outside a medieval walled city; the sun shone brightly overhead, and a crowd of people stood on the ramparts, cheering him on and welcoming him home. He felt comfortable and joyful.

When he was eventually brought back to consciousness in the hospital, he was upset. "I didn't want to leave. I liked going home," he said. "It was such a friendly place. I don't want to be here. That place felt more real."

Arthur's experience dovetails with other stories of crowds of angels or long-dead relatives or friends that I've heard from many people who were about to cross the great divide.

Arthur's story, however, is the only one I've heard that includes a walled city. Everybody's crossing is unique.

Several years later, Arthur got his wish: he crossed over and went home. No doubt his friends on the ramparts opened the gates and welcomed Arthur to his eternal abode.

Swing Low

Barry sat vigil at the hospital bedside of his dad, Marty, who was floating in and out of consciousness.

Suddenly Marty's expressionless face became animated. He opened his eyes and said, "The room's crowded, and they've all come to visit me."

Barry didn't see anyone. "Who's here, Dad?"

Marty stared at the corner of the room and began naming the long-dead relatives who'd come to welcome him home. "I can't rest because the room is so crowded," he complained. Then, arms outstretched, he reached upward and said, "What a beautiful chariot. It's come for me. Give me a ticket."

Barry saw no chariot. "I can't see it, Dad."

"It's right over there—it's bright gold," Marty insisted, as again he reached up with both hands. "I've got to go. Oh please, give me a ticket. I want to get on it. It's beautiful," he said. "It's beautiful."

Shortly afterward, Marty lapsed into a coma and died. He was smiling. Barry likes to think his dad got his ticket and went home on the golden chariot.

Chapter 6

God, Goddesses, and Other Archetypes

The love of heaven makes one heavenly.

William Shakespeare

As we have seen, otherworldly visitations occur when out-of-body souls appear to act as our helpers and guides, just as we earthlings act as guides for one another. Other visitors, called archetypal beings, arrive when people cry out for help in crisis situations. What is an archetype? It is a form or symbol that occurs throughout time and space and is a cross-cultural phenomenon. Among the archetypes that exist in human imaginations all over the globe: god, goddess, angel, demon, divine healer, divine or devilish destroyer, magician, warrior, hero, heroine, trickster, mermaid, wise fool, wise old crone, wise shaman, prophet, prophetess, wee people (goblins, trolls, fairies), priest, priestess, divine mother, divine maiden, divine son, divine father, dragon, the trinity, witch, and wizard. These beings show up in dreams, fairytales, myths, and legends in all cultures.

For instance, Mary, in addition to being Jesus's mother, can be viewed in her archetypal roles of the divine mother, the divine feminine, and divine purity. Symbolically speaking, both she and the Indian goddess Kali are examples of the divine mother in her "dark goddess" aspect—Mary in her guise as the Black Madonna, and Kali, a more ancient archetype, as the great Creator/Destroyer. Both are archetypal healers. The dark goddess is the goddess of fertility and procreation, allowing babies to be conceived and born, flora to flourish, fish to spawn, corn to grow, cattle to multiply, etc. In her most ancient forms (such as Kali and the Egyptian goddess Sekhmet), she is also the goddess of destruction and death, of cycles and seasons, of famine as well as fertility, and of plagues as well as healing.

In the masculine archetypal realm, the idea of a self-sacrificing god appears in many traditions. Jesus, the prime exemplar of divine self-sacrifice, offers his life to atone for the sins of others. His legacy is quite simple: "Love one another." His ascent into hell and his resurrection are archetypal events mirrored some four thousand years earlier in the Inanna myth (and in the Persephone myth, as well). According to Sumerian legend, Inanna, the queen of the universe, descended into and ascended from the netherworld to emerge armored with truth and the art of lovemaking.

In Greco-Roman tradition, the goddess Venus and the sun god Apollo epitomize divine love. Apollo, whose symbols include a bow and arrow (like Cupid's), was reputed to have rays of light radiating from his head, which sounds suspiciously like a halo. Apollo was the god of music, prophecy, healing, and poetry. The divine messenger Hermes/Mercury brought luck and sported wings on his heels to speed the message delivery process. A statue outfitted in a warrior's breastplate often represented Ares/Mars, the god of war. These archetypes appear in many cultures under different names.

Archetypes appear in visions and dreams because the dreamer requires very potent cosmic symbols and images far beyond the ordinary, and the dreamer's unconscious wants to grab his or her attention. Dreams containing archetypes are unforgettable. If you are interested in knowing more about archetypes, be sure to read the theories of Carl Jung or any of the Jungian depth psychologists, who have followed in his footsteps.

Darla's story is an example of a godly visit. As a teenager, Darla was diagnosed with Crone's disease. Once when she was home alone and in pain, she spontaneously began singing religious songs, both traditional hymns and inspirational popular songs. She sang for hours until, startled, she saw Christ's face appear on the wall. Darla heard him tell her not to worry—she'd be fine. The doctors finally got her illness under control, and now, twenty years later, she is fine, just as Jesus promised.

Enter the Beatles

While working on an autobiography, I was steeped in a chapter on the Virgin Mary. I felt her presence while writing about her, and, somewhat obsessed, I wrote between classes and grading student projects. After my 7:30 p.m. class, I rushed to meet my Ad Club students at the Seven Dragons Restaurant. I'd arranged for the students to help Elaine, the restaurant's owner, with an ad campaign. Grateful for their input, Elaine invited us to a seven-course Asian meal to let us experience her new chef's artistry and to show off her new karaoke machine.

When I arrived, my students were already enjoying the meal. Elaine said, "They're not doing karaoke. Why don't you sing? If you do, it'll break the ice, and the kids will start singing, too."

"Are you kidding?" I said. "I'm in no mood to sing right now. I'm exhausted!"

But Elaine insisted. She grabbed my arm, pulled me up onto the platform, and handed me a mike. "Sing!"

I looked at the video screen. The song that appeared there, out of the hundreds she could have chosen, was "Let It Be"! When I found myself singing about Mother Mary's "words of wisdom," I had to control my laughter. Mary appeared in my mind's eye, smiling.

Elaine was right: the kids did start stepping up to the mike. The Virgin Mary, as you can see, has a keen sense of humor—at least when she's dealing with me.

The Brain Thing

Florence visited her sister Jenny daily in the nursing home. Jenny, not quite fifty, was diagnosed with a glioblastoma, a particularly vicious cancerous brain tumor. The sisters, who were very close, had lost their mother to cancer just six months before, and they were still in mourning.

When Jenny was in the final stages of her illness, she chose to be in pain, instructing the hospice nurse to give her minimal medications because she didn't want to be "out of it" when her husband, family, and friends visited. I was her hospice chaplain, and I grew to know and love Jenny for her generosity of spirit, her lust for life, and her quick wit. The family gave her a lavish, loving fiftieth birthday party, and people from all parts of her life came to celebrate and say their final farewells.

Florence, continuing her daily visits, was understandably anxious and distressed watching her sister deteriorate, until Jenny said, "Flo, about this brain thing—I'm not worried anymore. Jesus sat there in the chair where you're sitting. He said I'd be fine." After Jesus's visit, the pain disappeared.

Two weeks later Jenny died peacefully, confident that Jesus was taking care of her, both in this world and the next.

Before Jenny's death, she and Florence had planned a memorial celebration. True to those plans, the celebration was held in a park, with food, drinks, and fun in abundance. Fred, a musician and longtime friend, played the guitar and sang Jenny's favorite songs. Jenny had made the favors that were laid out for all the attendees. She'd also chosen the games that were held throughout the day for children and adults and picked out the prizes awarded to the winners.

One by one, friends and relatives came forward, testifying to the joy Jenny had brought them, and I was privileged to lead a short memorial service for this remarkably positive woman. Knowing her enriched my life.

Lois's Source of Strength and Faith

My hospice patient Lois, who identified herself as a "nonpracticing Catholic," refused a priestly visit for the Anointing of the Sick (formerly called the Last Rites), but since she was deeply connected to the Virgin Mary, she asked me to join her in praying the Hail Mary. "I know I'm dying," Lois said. "She'll help me. Please keep praying to the Virgin after I can't do it for myself anymore."

"Lois, of course I'll say the Hail Marys," I said. "What brought you to such devotion?"

She smiled and said, "When I was younger, I bore seven children. Instead of getting easier, each labor was more excruciating than the one before. But what made those hard births bearable was the Virgin Mary appearing to me and helping me through all seven of them. She never let me down."

In Lois's old age, Mary remained her rock and her strength. When she lost consciousness, I continued praying to Mary, as she requested. Lois died smiling, and I believe Mary was there to greet her when she crossed the river, assisting in her rebirth.

In God's Hands

Martha, diagnosed with incurable breast cancer, was told she had three months to live. She went home and cried for hours. In the midst of her despair, she suddenly felt herself enfolded in the light-filled hands of God. Peace descended upon her, and calmed by his loving presence, she stopped crying. At that moment she began to accept her condition.

After entering hospice, she continued her smoking habit. ("Why not?" she'd say.) The nursing home's smoking room is located in the basement at the end of a long hallway, just past the hairdressing salon, whose large glass window allows passersby a full view of the patrons inside.

Several times when Martha walked past the salon, she saw her long-dead mother looking at her from the eyes of Janelle, a patient suffering from severe dementia. "It happens only when Janelle's hair is wrapped in large curlers," Martha told me. "She makes eye contact with me, and I swear my mother's eyes peer forth from a face that transforms and looks astoundingly like my mother's."

"Does Janelle look the same when you see her upstairs?" I asked.

"No!" she said. "I know it sounds goofy, but when I see Janelle in the dining room or in the hallway, with her hair properly coiffed, she looks nothing like my mom. It only happens when she's in curlers. Go figure!"

Whatever the explanation, Martha was comforted by those brief eye-to-eye and soul-to-soul encounters. Along with her profound encounter with God, they helped her deal with the effects of the cancer that finally took her life as predicted: three months after entering hospice, and shortly before her sixtieth birthday.

Kali Intervenes

Perhaps the time I was most severely tested was in 1993, when I discovered a lump in my breast. I was terrified, given my family history. Could it be "the big C"? After all, my mother died of cervical cancer, my grandfather of lung cancer, and my two aunts, one uncle, and three cousins of various forms of cancer. My fear was firmly based in reality.

I entered a state of denial: it was just another cyst. I watched it. It grew. The doctor said, "It's probably just another cyst. But let's take a mammogram and a biopsy, just to be sure." It was malignant.

"What are my choices?" I asked.

"You really have none," he said. "The lump's size and location make mastectomy the surgery of choice." Or, more accurately, the surgery of no choice.

I stormed, cried, agonized. But all the while I also felt guided, loved, and blessed. How strange, I thought, to experience ecstasy and pain simultaneously.

I had the mastectomy. I made some soothing audiotapes to be played in the operating room, and I instructed the anesthesiologist to give me positive suggestions about healing while I was under anesthesia. (He thought I was crazy, but he did it anyway.) I recovered quickly, exercised, felt good, and most important, felt guided throughout the process.

The next choice I confronted was whether or not to have chemotherapy. The turf wars went something like this:

Surgeon: "I got it all."

Oncologist: "You need the chemo." Then he scared me with sobering statistics. (Tough choice. Both brilliant men.)

I meditated. I read books. This was before computers, so the oncologist gave me a stack of medical journal articles. I got copies of my X-rays and my records. I became an expert on my ex-tumor, but I still couldn't decide. I read about Iscador, an alternative medicine derived from the female mistletoe tree. It looked promising, and I was lucky to find the right doctor to administer the shots; they required special training. I considered taking just the Iscador and foregoing the chemo, which frightened me.

A conversation over lunch with my friend Sydney, a Unitarian minister, helped clarify my choices. She said, "In the past five years I've had four friends with breast cancer. The two who chose only alternative medicine are dead." (Gulp!) "The other two are doing just fine. The one who reminds me most of you? She did both alternative and conventional therapies."

"How'd she deal with the chemo?" I asked. "It's putting poison in your body."

"She imagined that the fluids were the goddess Kali's healing energy flowing into her veins."

I liked that idea, but I still couldn't decide. So I went home. That night I couldn't sleep; I kept thinking about Kali, the very ancient Indian goddess. Finally I went into the living room, turned on the tube, and randomly chose a movie channel; it put me right to sleep. TV is, for me, the great drugless sleep maker.

I awoke at 4:00 a.m., that early-morning time when the veil between the worlds is very thin. On screen was a terrific actress, Ann Magnuson, portraying the goddess Kali. She was in a cave, embracing with her many arms a young pubescent boy-man whom, apparently, she was about to deflower. Really. (Just a short clip, it turned out, from what looked like a "must-miss" movie aimed at thirteen-year-old boys.) The tension dam burst. I laughed … and I laughed. Divine Wit exists, thank goodness.

Kali tweaked my funny bone and tickled my fancy. *I got it.* Kali was with me. Guiding me. In my corner. On my side.

So I did the chemo—and the alternative stuff. And I'm doing just fine. A bit lopsided, but fine.

Throughout the decision-making processes, and pre- and post-surgery, I was often in a transcendent state of ecstasy, although I experienced emotional (but remarkably little physical) pain. Sometimes I experienced both simultaneously; joy can exist in suffering. Because I had learned to listen to that still, small voice, I could respond to my soul's prompts. And I got by with a little help from my friends, embodied and disembodied. Sydney, there for a reality check, helped me decide on the chemo—and now, from a distance of twenty years, I see that it helped me to survive. Getting the Kali message was a cosmic wake-up call, saying, "Do it!" And to help with the healing process, people were praying for me all over the world. I was on several healing lists: Catholic, Sufi, Jewish, Buddhist, Hindu. Those earth-side healing angels worked hand in hand with my spiritual guidance system—prayer works!

Conclusion

Love alone is the fountain from which all virtues fall as drops of sparkling water.

Hazrat Inayat Khan

These stories show us the many different ways souls choose to communicate in this rich, multidimensional universe. Do we have explanations for all these events? Not really. I offer these tales because they happened; you can judge whether they resonate with your own experiences. What's clear to me is that consciousness survives, and love is the heavenly cord that connects us to our departed family and friends, transcending time and space. Souls retain their human personality and sense of humor. Many of them seem to enjoy playing with our senses—and so does God. Divine wit, as well as human wit, is evident in these tales.

If you haven't already done so, open your heart and mind—you, too, can have an exciting experience or two. A heavenly messenger, a disembodied friend or relative may be trying to reach you through your intuition, your dreams, or your five senses. As these stories suggest, there are many ways of knowing, so just stay open. And share your stories. When you do, you'll help heal yourself and others.